Discovered:
A New Shakespeare Sonnet
(or three, actually)

Also by Gilbert Wesley Purdy

POETRY

Mind Dance

NOVEL

Kafka in Richmond

NON-FICTION

Was Shakespeare Gay?
Straight Male Scholarly Angst and Shakespeare's Sonnets.

The Ties of the Railroad Tracks Home:
the Poetry of Jared Carter.

Henry David Thoreau and Two Other Autistic Lives:
before the diagnosis existed.

Edward De Vere was Shakespeare:
at long last, the proof.

Gilbert Wesley Purdy

Discovered:
A New Shakespeare Sonnet
(or three, actually)

V irtual

V anaprastha

Richmond, Virginia

Acknowledgments

This book would not have been possible without Google's wonderful determination to digitize millions of books, no longer under copyright, for free public use. The same may be said, especially in this instance, for the Early English Books Online/Text Creation Partnership (EEBO-TCP) which provided me a precise transcription of the key text from which citations are taken for this monograph. Their recent transition into a free access, highly dependable scholarly library was absolutely essential to this text and the discoveries it describes.

I would like to dedicate this book to Jeffrey and Tori Purdy, Allie and Emily Scott, the memory of my beloved parents, and to all of those living family members who have put up with me having my head constantly in a book and being otherwise incomprehensible.

Table of Contents

Introduction

Being supplied by Amazon with an easy means of independent publishing, and by Google Books and other digital libraries with the full texts of tens of millions of books published from the 15th to the early 20th centuries, it was a matter of course that territories once the sole province of academia would become open to the general public. The majority of the amateurs — the *lovers* — flooding into those territories were certain to be amateurs in the less complimentary sense of the word. In many ways, the expansion of access can only be unsightly and frustrating at the same time that it is liberating and glorious.

But our new digital resources also accelerate our passage through this frustrating transition. Eventually digital libraries would surpass the finest scholarly libraries of old in many ways. It was only a matter of time — and not a long time, by historical measure — until someone from entirely outside of the expected sphere — someone among the amateurs — made a discovery of the sort that was once rare if not impossible. Eventually, the independent publishing platform would make it possible to present to the world that exciting new discovery and many more to come.

This monograph is about one such discovery: a hitherto unattributed poem demonstrably written by William Shakespeare. I present strong and precise historical, statistical and comparative textual evidence, here, that three such poems exist in an obscure Elizabethan anthology of pirated manuscripts. One, however, is such a "slam dunk" that this monograph will deal in detail only with it. The others will receive limited mention: just enough to make a claim for them which will be further explored in subsequent monographs.

The Amazon audience, however, may not be ready just yet to support independent books that make demands upon a reader beyond a desire to be entertained or to be advised on matters of daily life in simple terms. To its advantage, this book is short. To its disadvantage, the evidence it presents cannot be simplified into easy reading before turning out the light for a good night's sleep. While that evidence fortunately reveals itself best as a detective story about how the pieces of an investigative puzzle came together, understanding the outcome of the investigation requires an investment of disciplined attention from the reader not generally essential to a detective story. Considerable rewrite will hopefully prove to have made each of the many aspects of the investigation as clear as possible.

By present measures I have still more unreasonable expectations that writing a book will retain some of the qualities I've always appreciated. I am not willing to surrender to the present demand the platform makes on its authors to spend vastly more time and money on advertising than were spent on writing and formatting the book itself. For all independent digital publishing has made it much easier to publish such books as this, it has made it much more difficult for them to be noticed among a flood of other books designed more as a ticket toward lottery-like profits through sensational subject matter, simplified texts and endless advertising campaigns.

On the other hand, I cannot rely on evaluation by an academic community whose livelihood is potentially threatened by the flood of amateurs such as myself. If they were to consider every such claim as this they would have time for little else. I will attempt to interest Shakespeare scholars in this discovery, with the understanding that they may find the possibility exciting, but cannot necessarily expect them to willingly participate in the transition that this undertaking represents — a transition that threatens in short order to limit the recognition and rewards available for their own scholarly products to the little I am likely to receive. In the growing flood of mainly pseudo-scholarship, all but the most fortunate swimmers, or most fearful waders, are likely to drown. The best available option is surely to apply for a floatation device (a grant), get clear of the churning waters, and hold on for dear life.

Add to this the fact that academia itself cannot agree on what specific tests suffice in order to assign an unattributed text to a particular author and the reader may understand the depth of my dilemma. Statistical analysis is widely agreed upon in general terms. My own statistical analysis, here, is by some measures more than sufficient, by others woefully lacking by virtue alone of the fact that it is being done by someone outside of academia.

No statistical evidence is likely to overcome the grand disqualifying factor, among academics, that I have previously written books on the Shakespeare authorship question. While I offer these as new poems by Shakespeare, without reference to the authorship question, Edward de Vere, the 17th Earl of Oxford, is one among the many characters unavoidably associated with this literary history. His name is associated with the pirated manuscripts among which the new Shakespeare sonnets are found. I have taken great care to avoid pointing to his role in the story as evidence in the authorship question. This is a monograph about three new Shakespeare poems. All else is incidental.

So then, given all of the impediments to getting this monograph before readers who might evaluate and appreciate it, I can only ask you, who have purchased or received a promotional copy, to be so kind as to give it a vitally important customer review. Should you find the book successful, please tell those potential customers who visit its Amazon book page as much and mention it to others among your friends and acquaintances who might be interested in its subject. The discovery is real, substantiated and so rare that perhaps three hundred years have passed without the like of it.

Where the Trail Begins

Like so much in late Elizabethan literature, the name "Thomas Nashe" is important and the best place to start this account. Nashe was born son of an impoverished "minister" in 1567. No record exists of the father having his own parish. Altogether eight children were born to the minister. Thomas and two others survived to adulthood.

In 1582, Nashe matriculated into St. John's College, at Cambridge University, as a sizar. The term "sizar" indicates that his family was too poor to pay the tuition and fees of the college. While he very probably had to perform menial tasks in lieu of his tuition, and would have been considered well below the social status of students whose families could afford to pay, a sizar was also a scholarship student. By one or more measures, he had already shown the intellectual talents that would bring him a brief, unstable but brilliant place in England's literary and intellectual history.

Nashe was further awarded a Lady Margaret Foundation grant in 1584. This, too, would have been a scholarship of sorts for academic excellence. Considering the fact that he would be able to remain at St. John's for 7 years without a fellowship, or other apparent source of income, the Lady Margret grant may have been renewed for each of his remaining 5 years.

When Nashe was finally cast forth from the college, London was crawling with writers of various stripes. The city was in the midst of a genuine literary renaissance. The competition was exciting, fierce and often vicious. Various references in his works and those of others make it likely that the highly social St. John's man already knew many if not most of the authors of the time and place. In 1589, not long after he had been shown the door at Cambridge, he was already sufficiently well known that he could be called upon to write an introduction to Robert Greene's pamphlet *Menaphon*. From among the younger writers, who would soon displace the old, he knew fellow Cambridge student Thomas Campion well. He spoke of Samuel Daniel and Matthew Roydon in terms that suggest appreciation and at least acquaintance. He would soon co-author the play *Dido of*

Carthage, with fellow Cambridge alum, and fellow scholarship student, Christopher Marlowe.[1]

Of the older generation, he knew John Lyly well and more than a few references in his works strongly suggest that he knew Lyly's old patron, the Earl of Oxford, almost as well. He knew Robert Greene perhaps the greatest of the London names at the time, best of all, and also Greene's arch-enemy Gabriel Harvey. Knowing Harvey and many of the young college men, he may also have made the acquaintance of the poet Edmund Spenser.

It must be admitted, however, that Thomas Nashe is almost completely silent about William Shakespeare. Only one possible reference to the London-based playwright or his works is to be found in any of Nashe's pages of any date and it is a famous reference to the play *Hamlet* made many years before the play is supposed to have been written. His opinion of the play is unclear given the passage of years and subsequent loss of context but he seems to have known it as a work so popular that lesser playwrights could not resist imitating it.

For all there was a renaissance, the writers of the time were paid only paltry sums for their work. They might receive a few extra pounds if they were lucky enough to find a patron. Toward the end of the reign of Elizabeth, however, paying patrons became fewer and farther between. Even Edward Spenser, whose epic poem *The Fairy Queen* would instantly become the most famous poem of the Queen's reign, and which was successfully dedicated to the Queen herself, received a Royal annuity of only £50 (approximately £10,000 or $15,000 in today's money). The amount was considered lavish by her Lord Treasurer. The rest of the writers of the time received much smaller one-time gifts if they were fortunate enough to receive patronage at all. The authors for the popular press and stage whose talents we so respect today generally lived from hand to mouth.

Nashe began his career by writing an introduction to *Menaphon*, a pamphlet by Robert Greene. Pamphlets themselves might receive about 40 shillings but Greene was so popular that he is sure to have received somewhat more. At best, then, Nashe received 40 shillings (which amounts to some $600) for his introduction. More likely he received the equivalent of $100-200 or even less.

---

[1] Marlowe was also a close friend of Roydon.

It is also likely that the introduction was his plum job at first. There can be little doubt that he collaborated on plays and pamphlets for which he was paid tiny amounts as a ghost writer and other such anonymous uses for his pen, wit and creative command of the university subjects he'd imbibed. He may also have participated in the petty criminal activities, or con-games, so common on the London streets at the time. The one thing of which we can be perfectly certain is that the amounts he might have earned from the occasional introduction alone could not possibly have kept him alive.

Being a particularly social type, and much desired for his good company, Nashe informs us in his own first pamphlet, *The Anatomy of an Absurdity*, that he stepped from Cambridge into the company of gentlemen:

> So it was, that not long since lighting in company with many extraordinarie Gentlemen, of most excellent parts, it was my chance (amongst other talke which was generally traversed amongst us) to moove divers Questions, as touching the severall qualities required in Castiglione[']s *Courtier*;...[2]

Nashe's survival as a writer likely depended as much, if not more, on his ability to provide entertaining company. He likely found himself treated to the occasional cheap meal, with wine or ale for beverage, at an "ordinary" (cheap restaurant), by those among the community who had means. Perhaps a week or a month beneath a friend's roof might come available. On these occasions the drink would flow and the carousers would pass around manuscripts of work not generally meant for publication. These details of the common writer's life were often written about at the time, in celebration and complaint, and would be referred to by Nashe himself in his satirical and highly amusing works.

By 1592, Nashe had replaced Greene as the most popular pamphleteer of the time. He himself was probably making somewhat more than the standard 40 shillings per effort. While the anonymous work still would have been a necessity, he had already reached the pinnacle of his profession. By the same year, he had already begun to test the limits of the profession so strenuously, in search of much needed income, that he was coming to the notice of the authorities.

---

[2] Nashe, *Complete*. Vol. 1 @ 8. "To the right Worshipfull Charles Blunt Knight, adorned with all perfections of honour or Arte,..." *The Anatomy of Absurdity*. London: Thomas Hackett, 1589.

On the occasion that concerns us, here, he wrote an introduction to an edition of Sir Philip Sidney's poem (actually, a sonnet sequence) *Astrophel and Stella*. The knight's was the only poem, at the time, with a reputation approaching that of *The Fairy Queen*. His romantic early death, while fighting with an English army in the low lands, had made it more popular still.

The introduction is even wilder than usual, and, by way of complimenting Sidney, pilloried London poetasters for having written and read abominably poorly. That does not concern us directly, however. What does concern us is that the volume included a collection of "sundry other rare sonnets of divers noble men and gentlemen," following Sidney's text. In the two instances where attributions are provided, these turn out to have been written by persons we know were Nashe's friends and associates. The suggestion is strong that, desperate as always for money, he had offered the printer private manuscripts, with which he had been entrusted during the nights carousing with the authors of the poems (or, perhaps, with mutual friends), for additional payment.

A note in the Stationers' Register, from shortly after the poems were published, informs us that the Baron of Burghley, Lord Treasurer, and principle advisor to the Queen, ordered that the volume quietly be called in and remaining copies destroyed.[3] This was speedily accomplished and Sidney's *Astrophel and Stella* later published without the poems by others and without hindrance from the Royal Court.

For this reason, *Syr P.S. His Astrophel and Stella. Wherein the excellence of sweete poesie is concluded. To the end of which are added, sundry other rare sonnets of divers noble men and gentlemen*, published in 1591, is among the rarest of Elizabethan books. It is possible that as few as two copies survive.

---

[3] Sidney, *Complete Poems*. Vol. 1 @ xxiv. " ...the Nash quarto of 1591 was certainly disapproved by some who claimed to interfere. The proof of this is found in the Stationers' Register, under the date of 18th September 1591, where we read: 'Item, paid to John Wolf, when he ryd with an answere to my L Treasurer, beinge with her majestie on progresse for the takinge in of bookes intituled Sir PS Astrophel and Stella.'"

The Excellence of Sweet Poesy

The "sundry other rare sonnets" were published in two groups. The first group consisted of 28 sonnets. On the page of the first sonnet appeared the inscription: "The Author of this Poeme, S. D." These are the initials of the poet Samuel Daniel as will soon be seen. The second consisted of 5 "cantos," or songs, followed by two miscellaneous poems. At the end of the five cantos proper appears the moniker "CONTENT". This is followed by the words "Megliora spero" ("I hope for better"). The next poem is followed by the only attribution in this section: "E.O.", the initials which Edward de Vere, the Earl of Oxford, used on the few occasions when he consented to have poems published under his own name.

The poem inscribed "E.O." is written in lines of eight iambic feet and reads as follows:

FAction that ever dwelles, in Court where wit excelles, hath set defiance.
Fortune and Love have sworne, that they were never borne, of one alliance.

Cupid which doth aspire, to be God of Desire, Sweares he gives lawes;
That where his arrowes hit, some joy, some sorrow it, Fortune no cause.

Fortune sweares weakest hearts (the bookes of Cupids Arts) turnd with hir wheele,
Sensles themselves shall prove: venter hath place in Love, aske them that feele.

This discord it be got Atheists, that honor not. Nature thought good,
Fortune should ever dwell in Court where wits excell, Love keepe the wood.

So to the wood went I, with Love to live and die, Fortune's forlorne:
Experience of my youth, made me thinke humble Truth In desarts borne.

My Saint I keepe to mee, and Joane her selfe is shee, Joane faire and true:
Shee that doth onely move passions of love with Love: Fortune adieu.[4]

Eight foot lines were rare but one other early poem[5] in the form is definitely attributed to Edward de Vere. Few poets display so many forms in such a

[4] Sidney. *A&S* (1591) @ 79-80.

[5] *Fuller's Worthies*. "Not Attaining to his Desire he Complainteth", Vol. 4 @ 48-9.

limited surviving sample of their work. The samples suggest that, early in his life, he regularly wrote songs in three and four foot lines as well as poems in iambic pentameter and six, seven and eight foot iambic lines.

The references to the Royal Court are also quite in place here with the attribution to Vere. He had been the Queen's favorite for some years until he got one of her ladies-in-waiting pregnant. From that time onward, he was *persona non grata*. After years attempting, without success, to get back into the Queen's good graces, he stopped attending at Court (where he once kept his own moveable set of apartments) unless he had specific business there.

Soon after his disgrace, Vere moved to London to be in the midst of the literary world he so loved and that so loved him. His first wife had been the daughter of the aforementioned Baron of Burghley. She died in 1588 while Edward, still disgraced, was away trying to get a commission to captain a ship against the Spanish Armada. Upon marrying his second wife, the two moved to Stoke Newington, a posh suburb north of London, where he was very much in the woods. Our volume of Sidney's *Astrophel and Stella* was published at around this time. Soon afterwards, he and his wife moved to her family estates in Hackney which was then a rural town of its own not yet incorporated into London.

The poem on the next page is the last in the volume and appears without attribution. I quote it in full:

> If flouds of teares could clense my follies past,
> And smokes of sighs might sacrifice for sin,
> If groning cries might salve my fault at last,
> Or endles mone for error pardon win;
> Then would I crie, weepe, sigh, and ever mone
> Mine error, fault, sins, follies past and gone.
>
> I see my hopes must wither in their bud,
> I see my favours are no lasting flowers,
> I see that words will breath no better good
> Than losse of time, and lightning but at howers:
> Then when I see, then this I say therefore,
> That favours, hopes, and words, can blinde no more.[6]

---

[6] Dowland. *Ayres*. 11.

Edward's sins and follies did not begin and end with a tryst with one of the Queen's ladies-in-waiting. The list is quite long. Nonetheless, he continued seeking favors from the Queen until her death, in 1603, none of which was ever granted. The themes of this poem, then, suggest that it also could be attributed to the Earl.

The poem was put to music and included in the *Second Book of Airs* (1600) by lutenist and composer John Dowland, however. It is not inconsistent with Dowland's style and its appearance in his book has led to its being attributed to him, probably correctly.

Printers were first and foremost businessmen; even more so in those days than now. Neither they nor their journeymen type-setters were as the rule literary types, or concerned that authors receive special treatment. The rights to literary works, when printing costs were not defrayed from the funds of the authors or their patrons, were purchased in perpetuity with a single payment. The author's interest was respected only inasmuch as he was a nobleman or his name could be expected to sell the book purchased. Not a whit more.

Anthologies were attractive for the fact that the text was generally collected from manuscript poems that still tended to be passed among the authors, their friends and associates. These manuscripts were not signed[7]. The authors retained no effective copyright therefore the text was acquired free of charge. If the printer/publisher knew who was the author of a particular poem there still might not appear an attribution. A single attribution among two or three or more poems by the same author, even if they were scattered in different locations, saved time and labor. What attributions appeared were often wrong, almost as often intentionally citing a more popular name than that of the actual author in an attempt to enhance sales.

So then, these "sundry other rare sonnets of divers noble men and gentlemen" bear only two sets of initials, and a single moniker or motto, each associated with certainty (if the journeyman typesetter had cared to make sure) only with the three individual poems that appear on the same

---

[7] The original manuscripts were frequently entered into the day books of various persons where they were sometimes ascribed to one or another author. These ascriptions were often the result of rumor and incorrect.

page. Moreover, without collaborative evidence, those three attributions cannot be considered 100% certain. These conditions are not unique to this book or these poems.

Another, far more famous, anthology reinforces these observations. As Mr. Charles Crawford pointed out in a 1908 number of the journal Notes and Queries[8], item #961 in Richard Allot's anthology *England's Parnassus* (1611) is ascribed to "E. O.". The poem is 18 lines long. The first 16 lines had previously been published by Robert Greene, as part of a poem entitled "Sonneto", in his *Menaphon* (1589).

More remarkable by far, for our purposes: the final two lines of the 18 line poem appear as the first two anonymous lines of "Canto Quarto"[9] from the miscellaneous poems at the end of the 1591 edition of *Astrophel and Stella*. Regarding *England's Parnassus*, #961[10], Crawford leans toward the theory that, during the printer's typically careless hurry to have the page set, Greene's name was left off and the lines were combined with two separate lines, by another author, which were supposed to follow it.

---

[8] Crawford, Charles. *Notes and Queries, Tenth Series, Volume IX*, May 2, 1908. "Englands Parnassus, 1600." 341-2.

[9] Sidney, *A&S* (1591) @ 78.

> **LOve whets the dullest wittes, his plagues be such,**
> **But makes the wise by pleasing doat as much.**
> So wit is purchast by this dire disease,
> Oh let me doat, so Love be bent to please.

[10] *Englands Parnassus*. #961 @ 131.

> Love is a discord and a strange divorce,
> Betwixt our sence and rest, by whose power,
> As mad with reason, we admit that force,
> Which wit or labour never may divorce.
> It is a will that brooketh no consent.
> It would refuse, yet never may repent.
> Love's a desire, which for to waight a time,
> Doth loose an age of yeares, and so doth passe,
> As doth the shadow severd from his prime,
> Seeming as though it were, yet never was,
> Leaving behind, nought but repentant thoughts,
> Of dayes ill spent, of that which profits noughts.
> It's now a peace, and then a sudden warre,
> A hope consumde before it is conceiv'd,
> At hand it feares, and menaceth a farre,

But Crawford doesn't stop there. He declares that the assignment to E.O. is clearly erroneous because the final two lines are not ascribed to E.O. in the 1591 edition of *Astrophel and Stella*. If not inscribed "E.O." in the earlier volume, he maintains, then Allot had wrongly recalled the attribution from memory rather than having been informed of it from other quarters. Allot, or Matthew Roydon (the man Crawford himself argues must have been Allot's friend), or another such associate, however, may easily have supplied the true ascriptions from better information than appeared in the pirated portion of the 1591 *Astrophel and Stella*.

Considering the fact that Roydon's associate, Nashe, is far and away the likeliest source for the manuscripts that provided the printer of the *Astrophel and Stella* of 1591 with the "sundry other rare sonnets of divers noble men and gentlemen," he would have been among the persons through whose hands many if not all of the original manuscripts had passed. Furthermore, Allot was often enough correct that his anthology is generally considered a valuable source of attribution. Given these facts, Crawford's assertion is questionable at the very least. Moreover, the moniker "CONTENT", to which Crawford assigns all of the cantos, denying any competing claims, appears only after the "Canto Quinto".

Crawford's next most likely alternative explanation was that Greene, like nearly all pamphleteers, (and Greene was more egregious than most,) had included the poem in *Menaphon* as his own in order to have his manuscript to the printer's in time to receive the money for his evening's supper[11]. About this I cannot express an informed opinion, but about the final two lines it can resoundingly be said that they were neither written nor stolen at any time by the old pamphleteer.

If we accept Crawford's theory that the poems were run together (and I do), we are left with an ascription indicating that two lines of "Canto

---

And he that gaines, is most of all deceiv'd.
Love whets the dullest wits his plagues be such,
But makes the wise by pleasing, dote as much.
EO

[11] I've added the colorful supper image to expand upon Crawford's "Poor Robert Greene has much to answer for, since we know he was a notorious filcher of other men's work."

Quarto", from the "sundry other rare sonnets" at the end of the 1591 edition of *Astrophel and Stella*, are attributed elsewhere (in a very famous Elizabethan anthology as carelessly printed as most) to "E.O." These are the same initials to which a poem is ascribed, two pages later. As in so many literary matters Elizabethan, however, 100% certainty is simply not possible.

Less confusing would seem to be that fact, first brought to light in a second letter by Crawford[12], that #1174, in Allot's *England's Parnassus*[13], ascribed to "E. of Ox.", is identical to the second stanza of "Canto Quinto"[14] ("the fifth song") among the "sundry other rare sonnets of divers noble men and gentlemen" at the back of our *Astrophel and Stella* of 1591. Item #115 is identical to the third stanza. The 1611 Allot anthology would seem to clearly show us that Edward de Vere, the Earl of Oxford, was asserted to be the author of at least these additional lines from "Canto Quarto" and "Canto Quinto". All of this appears immediately preceding another poem, appearing only in the 1591 *Astrophel and Stella*, inscribed with Oxford's standard initials.

---

[12] *Notes and Queries, Tenth Series, Volume IX*, August 1, 1908, 84-5.

[13] *Englands Parnassus.* #1174 @ 157.

> What plague is greater then the griefe of minde?
> The griefe of mind that eates in every vaine:
> In every vaine that leaves such clods behind,
> Such clods behind as breed such bitter paine.
> So bitter paine that none shall ever finde
> What plague is greater then the griefe of minde.

[14] Sidney, *A&S* (1591). @ 79.

> VVhat plague is greater than the griefe of minde,
> The griefe of minde that eates in everie vaine,
> In everie vaine that leaves such clods behind,
> Such clods behinde as breed such bitter paine,
> So bitter paine that none shall ever finde,
> What Plague is greater than the griefe of minde.

Of Canons and Scholars

But not every complication in these matters is due to Elizabethan pamphleteers and printers. In 1906 a fateful passage appeared in a volume on the Elizabethan author Abraham Fraunce, by G. E. Moore Smith[15].

> Hunter in his *Chorus vatum* (British Museum *Additional MSS.* 24488) makes the statement (echoed by Mr. Sidney Lee in his life of [Abraham] Fraunce in the *Dictionary of National Biography*): "There are five songs by him in Sir Philip Sidney's *Astrophel and Stella*, 1S91." The songs referred to, as Mr. Lee tells me, are those called "Canto primo" "Canto secundo" "Canto tertio" "Canto quarto" and "Canto quinto", signed "Content. Megliora spero".

Joseph Hunter and Sidney Lee are among the brightest lights of 19th and early 20th century Elizabethan scholarship. Their combined weight might seem to settle the matter once and for all. But however much Lee did correct the record and make "Megliora spero" part of the moniker that follows "Canto Quinto" rather than the title of the Earl of Oxford's poem, on the next page[16], he was ill-informed in the rest of his opinion.

Much to Moore Smith's credit, with the help of another fine scholar, Henry Bullen, he saw the error in Hunter and Lee's attribution:

> The first [canto], "Harke all you Ladies that doo sleepe" is undoubtedly Campion's and is found in his *Booke of Ayres* 1601[17] and in Mr. Bullen's edition of Campion, 1889, p. 21. Mr. Bullen writes to me that he has no doubt that the third "My

---

[15] Fraunce. @ xxxviii.

[16] Most, if not all, scholars of the 1591 *Astrophel and Stella* declare that "Canto Quinto" was followed by the moniker "CONTENT" and the title of the poem on the following page was "Megliora spero". In the original text, however, the motto "CONTENT. Megliora spero" appears entirely at the end of "Canto Quinto". As is the case of all of the "sundry other rare sonnets," the poem on the next page has no title.

[17] Campion. *Works* @16.

Love bound me with a kisse" is also Campion's. With regard to the second "What faire pompe have I spide of glittering ladies" (the only one by the way which is in a classical metre) Mr. Bullen says "it is a lovely bit of versification far beyond the reach of lumbering Abraham Fraunce". In fact there seems no reason whatever for assigning any of these poems to Fraunce and every reason for assigning the whole group to Campion.[18]

On the debit side, apparently unaware of the attribution of parts of the cantos to the Earl of Oxford, Moore Smith has expanded on Bullen's Campion attribution, simply because he *felt* there was "every reason" for assigning all of the cantos at the end of the *Astrophel and Stella* of 1591 to Campion. He appears never to have enlightened us as to what "every reason" specifically amounted. Campion only republished the "Canto Primo", making no claim whatsoever to the others, establishing a presumption that he had not written the other four: a presumption that more than one person wrote the five cantos.

Future scholars would accept Moore Smith's *feeling* until it would become an unquestioned "fact" of the canon. Percival Vivian, the editor of the next new collection of the works of Campion[19], would "discover" additional reasons to attribute the cantos in their entirety to the object of his scholarly research. Mr. Bullen's original position, for all it is the only precisely correct position, was left behind, as the Campion attribution of all of the cantos (however wrong it was and remains) became resoundingly established "fact".

To establish unfounded assumptions more firmly still, Charles Crawford's two letters to *Notes and Queries*, mentioned above, were a preliminary to his publishing a now standard 1913 edition of *Englands Parnassus* (from which we have already quoted). In his edition he firmly repeated that *all* E.O. attributions in *Englands Parnassus* had been carelessly *mis*-taken from the poems at the end of the 1591 *Astrophel and Stella*.

---

[18] Fraunce @ xxxviii

[19] Campion. *Works*, l-li @ l. "Some of the poems in this volume have not been previously included in the canon of Campion's works; the authenticity of these, therefore, and some others I propose to consider before proceeding to discuss the verse itself."

For two other extracts from the poems in the 1591 quarto, signed 'Content', see Nos. 962 and 1174, which *E.P.* likewise wrongly ascribes to the Earl of Oxford, whose contribution, entitled *Megliora spero*, follows in the quarto immediately after the poems by 'Content'.[20]

There would seem to be *every reason* to suspect that Percival Vivian felt confirmed in his position regarding the cantos because it was consistent with Crawford's letters to *Notes and Queries*, and that Crawford in turn felt confirmed by the "discovery" declared by Vivian in his *Campion's Works* of 1909. Both books issued from the same Clarendon Press.

But the 1591 *Astrophel and Stella* had been called-in almost immediately after it was released. The likelihood that Richard Allot, editor/publisher of *Englands Parnassus* possessed a copy 20 years later is quite low. And if he did somehow possess a copy, the strength of Crawford's claim that Allot had selected a few disembodied lines from the poems in question and mistakenly attributed them to E.O., comes foremost from a 1906 canonical attribution, by Percival Vivian, of all five of the cantos to Thomas Campion — an attribution founded upon Moore Smith's earlier *feeling*.

Voila! Allot's source has been created whole cloth nearly 300 years after the fact. The *feeling* planted by G. E. Moore Smith, two years earlier, has bloomed into the exciting "discovery" of Percival Vivian, which has established the canonical position in the field. This "discovery" has supported Charles Crawford's position, while it has been, at the same time, in no small part encouraged by Crawford's own preliminary work. It all has further supported his position that, as a matter of consistency, Allot can only have misremembered the E.O. ascriptions that appeared in *Englands Parnassus*, from out of the 1591 *Astrophel and Stella* where they bore no E.O. ascriptions to begin with. Everyone's résumé has been updated with nifty new entries. Only, there is not a shred of verifiable evidence that Campion wrote any but the first canto; nor that Allot excerpted lines for his anthology from the "sundry other rare sonnets" and incorrectly remembered the author of certain lines from the "Canto Quinto" as the Earl of Oxford.

In 2002, Frank Davis, MD, contributor and editorial board member to The Oxfordian, a journal of Shakespeare authorship studies, addressed the

---

[20] *Englands Parnassus* @ 392 fn.

Campion attribution of the five cantos in his paper on "The Poem Grief of Minde: Who Wrote It?"[21] Dr. Davis objected to the attribution of all of the cantos to Campion based upon reasons similar to those I have presented[22]. While I cannot agree with the doctor that general textual comparison is sufficient basis to assert the authorship of the Earl of Oxford (and much more), the examples in the essay are suggestive.

Under the subheadings "Wrongly Attributed" and "Similarity of versification vs. close translation" he mentions Percival Vivian's claim that all of the anonymous cantos were verifiably by Campion because near-translations had been found in Campion's Latin poems. (Campion was as much a Latin language poet as an English.) Thus, according to Vivian, Campion did later republish/claim all of the cantos in his own books after a fashion.

Dr. Davis provides originals and translations of the supposed Latin parallels and skillfully demonstrates that Vivian had merely seen what he wished to see. The purported near-translations amount to nothing more than such similarities as one would expect between any two poems on similar themes — themes quite common among all poets of the time. Vivian saw what he needed to see in order to have a discovery to his name.

My understanding of the present state of the matter should be obvious. Thomas Campion is the author of the "Canto Primo". This is clear from the *fact* that he reprinted the poem ten years later in his first book of English language poems, *First Booke of Ayres* (1601). Campion was not in the least shy about seeing his work in print under his own name. He regularly published books and anthology pieces in English and Latin, as well as masques. In *fact*, he was an eagerly public poet who left little if any of his work unpublished. The *fact*, then, that he did not publish the other four cantos strongly suggests that they did not come from his pen. The *fact* that some part of the remaining cantos are ascribed to the Earl of Oxford elsewhere in a renowned anthology only normally prone to errors, makes him the prime candidate for having written those lines. The remaining lines were either meant to remain private or were otherwise abandoned by one or another of the men or belong to someone else yet to be discovered.

---

[21] Davis, 159-173.

[22] I was pointed in the direction of much of the information I've provided above by Dr. Davis's paper.

Returning to Mr. Davis's paper, then, he does make the intriguing observation that a close variation upon the image to "seale a kisse" in the "Canto Secundo", appears in Shakespeare's *Measure for Measure*. In fact, the image appears in a number of Shakespeare plays. We find the lines from *Measure for Measure* in a song at the beginning of Act IV scene i:

> But my kisses bring again
> Seals of love, but seal'd in vain…

The song is written in Venus and Adonis stanza with iambic tetrameter lines. That is to say: it is a lyric poem within the text of the play. In the play *King John* (II. i. lines 19-20) we find:

> Upon thy cheek I lay this zealous kiss,
> As seal to this indenture of my love.

When Pandarus speaks the following lines to Troilus and Cressida, in the play of that name (III. iii. lines 182-3), he is calling upon the characters to kiss:

> Go to, a bargain made! seal it, seal it;
> I'll be the witness.

Following this official seal upon the agreement, he directs the two to an available "chamber with a bed".

Be this as it may, no foundation is laid for this line of pursuit, in the doctor's paper, and it is not pursued further. If pursued on such general terms, also, the expanded list of uses Shakespeare made of the image would still be no more than intriguing. Other poets from the time used similar images, if not precisely the same.

More importantly, still, for present purposes, Dr. Davis has not quoted what will turn out to be by far the most important instance in which Shakespeare uses the kiss-as-seal metaphor. At lines 511-16 of the long poem *Venus and Adonis*, its publication still some year-and-a-half in the future when the 1591 *Astrophel and Stella* appeared, we find the following:

> Pure lips, sweet seals in my soft lips imprinted,
> What bargains may I make, still to be sealing?"

To sell myself I can be well contented,
So thou wilt buy, and pay, and use good dealing.
What purchase if you make for fear of slips,
Set thy seal-manual on my wax-red lips.[23]

It is these lines that will soon prove to be all to the point and only marginally as the result of the kiss-as-seal image.

To finish with Mr. Davis's interesting paper, then, he ends with a reflection on the parallels of medical knowledge he finds in the cantos and in the work of the Earl of Oxford. His findings are limited in the face of the small sample sizes available to him.

On this occasion, however, Dr. Davis might have been better served if he had taken a law degree. In the first stanza of "Canto Quinto", from which "Grief of Minde" forms the second stanza, a far more striking (shocking even) connection to the plays of William Shakespeare lies hidden in plain sight: the word "arbitrement".

A Daie, a night, an houre of sweete content,
Is worth a world consum'd in fretfull care,
Unequall Gods in your *Arbitrement*
To sort us daies whose sorrowes endles are,
And yet what were it? as a fading flower;
To swim in blisse, a daie, a night, an hower.

Few, if any, single words are as indicative of Shakespeare as this one. Neither I nor the Google search engine are aware of any other author of poems, plays or novels who has ever employed the word in his or her texts. Centuries before, Chaucer used it once in a prose work. Francis Bacon used it occasionally in professional works specifically about the law (as did others). The only author — bar none, other than the author of the first stanza of "Canto Quinto" — to employ it, then or since, in a poem, play or novel was William Shakespeare.

In *King Lear* (IV. Viii. Lines 94-5), the Earl of Kent speaks with a gentleman retainer:

---

[23] Shakespeare. *Poems* @ 26.

Kent. Report is changeable. 'Tis time to look about; the powers
of the kingdom approach apace.
Gent. The arbitrement is like to be bloody.

In *Twelfth Night* III. Iv. 271-4, we have the word put to lighter uses in a
comedy. Viola speaks with Fabian:

Vio. Pray you, sir, do you know of this matter?
Fab. I know the knight is incensed against you, even
to a mortal arbitrement; but nothing of the
circumstance more.

In part 1 of *King Henry IV* (IV. i. lines 69-73), Worchester regrets the failure
of the Earl of Northumberland to join with the rebel force, marching to meet
King Henry, as agreed:

For well you know we of the offering side
Must keep aloof from strict arbitrement,
And stop all sight-holes, every loop from whence
The eye of reason may pry in upon us:...

To close out the list, I provide the appropriate citations from Shakespeare's
plays *Cymbeline* (I. iv. lines 4-8), *Richard III* (V. iii. lines 88-90) and *King
Henry V* (IV. i. lines 167-75), respectively:

Faith, yes, to be put to the arbitrement of swords; and by such
two that would; by all likelihood; have confounded one the
other, or have fallen both.

*

Prepare thy battle early in the morning,
And put thy fortune to the arbitrement
Of bloody strokes and mortal-staring war.

*

Besides, there is no king, be his cause never so spotless, if it
come to the arbitrement of swords, can try it out with all
unspotted soldiers: some peradventure have on them the guilt
of premeditated and contrived murder; some of beguiling
virgins with the broken seals of perjury; some, making the

wars their bulwark, that have before gored the gentle bosom
of peace with pillage and robbery.

Again, not only is the word a particular favorite of Shakespeare, in his
plays, but it is used by him alone, except, perhaps, for our single instance in
the first stanza of "Canto Quinto". Or perhaps this is not an exception but
rather an addition to the above list.

Two details, it must be admitted, in order to show appropriate scholarly
balance, differ between the example from the Shakespeare canon and the
stanza before us. First, none of the examples from Shakespeare comes from
a poem. Second, only in "Canto Quinto" is the arbitrement between the
gods rather than humans.   The second detail seems certainly
inconsequential. The first is not necessarily so. But neither could possibly
put a proper scholarly bloodhound off so promising a scent.

It also is unlikely that the mere presence of the word "arbitrement,"
stunning though it is, is strong enough to assign the stanza or the entire
canto to Shakespeare. An exciting discovery seemed so tantalizingly close.
I had not yet read all of the "sonnets" yet, however. Reading "Canto
Quinto" the odds seemed quite high that there might be something more —
much more — to be found not far off.

The Game is Afoot

It may be recalled that the cantos we have been vetting are only one of two sections of "sundry other rare sonnets" added to the end of the 1591 *Astrophel and Stella*. The other section is composed of 28 poems more properly called "sonnets" by present definition. They are poems of 14 lines with one or another of two traditional rhyme schemes. Specifically, 26 are what we now call "Shakespearean sonnets" and two are "Petrarchan sonnets".

The next year, the poet Samuel Daniel published the first quarto of his now famous sonnet sequence *Delia*. He began a letter dedicating the volume to Sir Philip Sidney's sister, the Countess of Pembroke, with an explanation:

> Right honorable, although I rather desired to keep in the private passions of my youth, from the multitude, as things utterd to my selfe, and consecrated to silence: yet seeing I was betraide by the indiscretion of a greedie Printer, and had some of my secrets betraide to the world, uncorrected, doubting the like of the rest, I am forced to publish that which I never ment.[24]

This complaint about having his poems stolen was a good excuse to fulfill his desire to publish while maintaining the pose of a gentleman, above the fray, not a common poet publishing his own work during his lifetime. The publishing did not stop there, however, regardless that no further poems were stolen, and it is unlikely that Daniel would have kept his poems private for much longer even had they not been pirated. Samuel Daniel was an exceptional poet who did not hesitate to publish everything he wrote throughout a 30 year career.

All 28 sonnets in the first section of the "sundry other rare Sonnets" appear in editions of Daniel's *Delia* to this day. Generally, when the earlier

---

[24] Daniel. *Works*, I. 33.

appearance in *Astrophel and Stella* is mentioned, editors state outright that the sonnets all were taken from the text of his *Delia*. At times the number of sonnets is tallied at 26, 24, at times 28. In an attempt to understand these discrepant figures I sought further details.

The disgraced Elizabethan scholar, and forger, John Payne Collier, it turns out, published the closest thing we possess to a facsimile of the 1592 *Delia* first quarto. It is the completely and verifiably genuine text. Working from the original, he discovered that several of the *Astrophel and Stella* sonnets uniformly included in later editions of *Delia* and Daniel's collected poems did not actually appear in either the first edition of *Delia* or any edition of any book by Daniel published during his lifetime.

> We add, for the purpose of recognition, the first lines of four sonnets which are given by Newman[25] to Daniel, and which we do not recollect to have met with elsewhere.
>
> "The onely bird alone that Nature frames" &c
>
> "The slie Inchanter, when to worke his will" &c
>
> "The tablet of my heavie fortunes here" &c
>
> "Way but the cause, & give me leave to plaine me" &c[26]

This is the source of the discrepant claims as to the number of sonnets in the 1591 edition of *Astrophel and Stella* which appeared the next year in the first quarto of Samuel Daniel's *Delia*. The answer is that 24 of the "sundry other rare sonnets" appear in *Delia*, four do not. Nor do any of the four appear in any edition of the highly popular *Delia*, nor any volume of any other work, during Daniel's lifetime. After Daniel's death, however, the sonnets began to be attributed to him without explanation.

The pattern is a recognizable one. In his *The Complete Works in Verse and Prose of Samuel Daniel*, the exceptional Elizabethan scholar Alexander

---

[25] Thomas Newman was the printer of the 1591 edition of *Astrophel and Stella*.

[26] Daniel. *Delia* @ ii.

Grossart accepted the traditional assignment of the sonnets to Daniel's pen, thereby establishing what would be the Daniel canon to this day.

> Sonnet 17 is the fourth and last of the Sonnets given by Newman and Nashe, but not reprinted by Daniel albeit as certainly his.[27]

But why is it "certainly his"? Because Grossart is an expert and he had a *feeling?* The attribution is not based on any further evidence than the facts that the poem appeared among the "sundry other rare sonnets" at the back of the 1591 *Astrophel and Stella* and that he has a *feeling* that *all* the sonnets there "certainly" belong to Daniel. Daniel himself, however, seems not to have shared Grossart's *feeling.* Again, there is not a shred of evidence that any of the poems that Daniel did not choose to publish under his name were written by him. During his life, he published everything he felt worthy of the press, at least, and at least one of the four additional sonnets is arguably far better written than those Daniel chose to publish in *Delia.*

But matters are even more exemplary, in this instance, of the flawed scholarship of which even exceptional scholars are capable in their hurry to churn out material. After reading Grossart's notes on the four sonnets, it is clear that he did not have the original 1591 edition before him. He was working from transcriptions and the transcriptions were incorrect. His numbering is different than the original.[28] The first sonnet never published by Daniel, however, is numbered the same in the volume and by Grossart's accounting. It is sonnet number 3:

> Sonnet 3 was not reprinted by Daniel but asserts its authorship. It is as follows:—

The onely birde alone that Nature frames,
When weary of the tedious life shee lives,
By fier dies, yet finds new life in flames:
Her ashes to her shape new essence gives,
For haplesse loe even with mine owne desires
I figured on the table of my hart,

---

[27] Daniel. *Works* @ 28.

[28] This is understandable as the numbering in the 1591 edition is not sequential and he (or his transcriptionist) chose to use sequential numbering however much it might confuse matters.

The goodliest shape that the worlds eye admires,
And so did perish by my proper arte.
And still I toyle to change the Marble brest
Of her whose sweete Idea I adore,
Yet cannot finde her breath unto my rest;
Hard is her heart, and woe is me therefore.
O blessed he that joyes his stone and arte,
Unhappie I to love a stonie harte.[29]

The problem with this sonnet goes much deeper than numbering, however. Only the first four lines of it belong to sonnet 3. The final 10 lines actually appear in Daniel's *Delia* as the final 10 lines of sonnet 7. It is impossible to know what Grossart might have meant by "asserts its authorship" but if he meant that lines from sonnet 3 appear elsewhere in Delia, his impression comes from the erroneous transcription of his text. This simply is *not* the text of Sonnet 3.

The actual text of Sonnet 3 reads as follows:

The onely bird alone that Nature frames,
When weary of the tedious life shee lives,
By fier dies, yet finds new life in flames,
Hir ashes to hir shape new essence gives.
When onely I the onely wretched wight,
Wearie of life that breaths but sorrows blasts,
Pursues the flame of such a beautie bright,
That burnes my heart, and yet my life still lasts.
O Soveraigne light that with thy sacred flame
Consumes my life, revive me after this,
And make me (with the happie bird) the same
That dies to live, by favour of thy blisse.
This deede of thine shall shew a Goddesse power,
In so long death, to grant one living hower.

Without careful study, it could easily be attributed to any of the half-dozen most talented sonneteers of the time (of which Daniel was one). Without such study there is no way to assert that the sonnet itself "asserts its authorship". Grossart's uncharacteristically shoddy work, here, and his

---

[29] Daniel. *Works*, I. 25-6.

obvious hurry, strongly suggest that he did not engage in such careful study.

From this and the other transcriptions available to Grossart, he has had a *feeling*. I will show that, in at least one instance (and probably three), his *feeling* was almost certainly wrong. In that one instance, the sonnet was almost certainly written by the only creative writer to use the word "arbitrement" in his creative works. For similarly compelling textual reasons, the sonnet was almost certainly written by William Shakespeare.

The sonnet labeled "Sonnet 16," at the back of the 1591 edition of *Astrophel and Stella*, corresponds to Grossart's Sonnet 17. The differences in his text are few and resoundingly minor. As we have noted above, he provides the following assessment:

> Sonnet 17 is the fourth and last of the Sonnets given by Newman and Nashe, but not reprinted by Daniel albeit as certainly his.

Whether Grossart's aforementioned blunder as to Sonnet 3 has helped him be certain or not, it does indicate that he was not being thorough in his evaluation. Rather than provide his slightly altered text of Sonnet 16, I give the following carefully transcribed from the original volume and verified correct:

> Way[30] but the cause, and give me leave to plaine me,
> For all my hurt, that my harts Queene hath wrought it,
> Shee whom I love so deare, the more to paine me,
> Withholds my right, where I have dearely bought it.
> Dearely I bought that was so highly rated,
> Even with the price of bloud and bodies wasting,
> Shee would not yeeld that ought might be abated,
> For all shee saw my Love was pure and lasting.
> And yet now scornes performance of the passion,
> And with hir presence Justice overruleth,
> Shee tels me flat hir beauty beares no action,
> And so my plee and proces shee excludeth:

---

[30] Weigh

> What wrong shee doth, the world may well perceive it,
> To accept my faith at first, and then to leave it.

Regardless of Grossart's confidence, this sonnet is very different from any that Daniel would ever write. At the same time, it displays signature traits throughout traditionally associated with William Shakespeare.

Those who know the sonnets of both Daniel and Shakespeare well know that they are in many ways remarkably alike — arguably, more so than any two English poets alive in the late 1580s or early 1590s. The relationship between their authors' respective plays about Anthony and Cleopatra, makes it still more clear that each was aware of and borrowed from the other's work. But there are also definite differences between them, differences that make clear that this sonnet was not written by Samuel Daniel but by William Shakespeare.

Texts and Tables

While we as readers might *feel* that the sonnet is more or less like other sonnets by Shakespeare or Daniel, this *feeling* is of only the most limited determinative value. Once we are presented with a sonnet that *feels* Shakespearean, the next step must be to investigate the vocabulary and specialized usages in the sonnet that may be indicative of the author. If two poets appear to be the only two in question, a close comparison between their works may make clear which of the two wrote the poem. Nevertheless, comparing the texts of Shakespeare to Daniel does not amount to an exhaustive comparison of all sonneteers writing at the time.

If we set aside all of the vocabulary from the above poem that are common to all authors of the time (articles, pronouns, prepositions, common adjectives and adverbs, etc.), the words that remain are something of a vocabulary fingerprint. The following Table 1 provides the list of less common words of Sonnet 16 and the number of occurrences in the collective plays and poems of both William Shakespeare and Samuel Daniel. The counts for Shakespeare's plays are taken from *The Complete Concordance to Shakespeare* (1878) by Mary Cowden Clark. The counts for Shakespeare's poems are taken from *A Concordance to Shakespeare's Poems* (1875) by Mrs. Horace Howard Furness. The counts for Daniel are taken from exhaustive Google book searches on volumes 1 through 3 of *The Complete Works of Verse and Prose of Samuel Daniel* edited by Alexander Grossart. As we have no prose from Shakespeare, apart from prose sections in his plays, Daniel's literary prose is not included.

The exact grammatical form of the words is shown in the unshaded rows, in accordance with unconditioned statistical analysis. The shaded rows provide word counts for close variants, selected to highlight facts about the unconditioned exact word. All spellings of the word, at the time, have been counted and entered in the table under a single standardized modern spelling.

The first notable fact is that all but two words appear elsewhere in the vocabulary of the poems and plays of Shakespeare, all but five in the poems and plays of Daniel. While the Bayesian statistical approach of Thisted and Efron[31] has been largely refuted as a tool for identifying Shakespeare authorship, its manner of calculating the rate at which new words might appear in reputed Shakespeare texts has been supported by Eric Sams and Robert Matthews[32]. The number of new words (based strictly upon identical grammatical form) that might be expected in a Shakespeare poem of this length according to both Thisted and Sams is 2.09.

For two of these words, ending in the old "–eth" third person present-indicative tense, I have adhered to the old grammatical form. Both poets rarely used this old-style of the tense but they did use it from time to time. Neither poet ever used these specific words in this particular tense. By itself, this finding need not argue for or against the authorship of one or the other. Only a persistent, accumulative pattern of vocabulary more in accordance with the body of work of either man can be considered determinative. The greater the differential, the likelier the identification of the sonnet with one or the other author.

The texts of the poems and plays of each man are not equivalent in all respects. First, Daniel's work is made up much more from poems, much less from plays. The opposite is the case with Shakespeare: his text is taken much more from plays, less from poems. Between the two, Daniel's works are more balanced between the two genres. This should make little difference, statistically speaking. Nevertheless, I have provided separate vocabulary counts from poems and plays for each author. The higher combined count for each word on this core list is given in brackets.

---

[31] Thisted, Ronald. "Did Shakespeare Write a Newly Discovered Poem?" Technical Report No. 111. Stanford, California: Stanford Universtiy, April 1986. https://statistics.stanford.edu/sites/default/files/BIO%20111.pdf

[32] Sams, Eric. "On the use of Thisted & Efron's technique to determine authorship." http://ericsams.org/index.php/shakespeare-archive/essays-and-reviews-unpubl/262-on-the-use-of-thisted-efron-s-technique-to-determine-authorship.

Table 1: Shakespeare-Daniel Raw Vocabulary Comparison (Pt 1)

Vocabulary Word	Shakespeare			Daniel			notes
	Plays	Poems	Total	Plays	Poems	Total	
Abated	3	0	[3]	1	1	2	
Abate	13	1	[14]	1	4	5	
Action	112	5	[117]	10	24	34	
Bought	52	1	[53]	2	6	8	
Dearly bought	1	0	1	2	3	[5]	
Dearly	32	1	[33]	7	6	13	
Excludeth	0	0	0	0	0	0	
Flat	29	0	[29]	1	2	3	Neither has "flat" for "flatly"
Hurt	84	4	[88]	16	12	28	
Lasting	12	4	[16]	1	6	7	
Overruleth	0	0	0	0	0	0	
Perceive	89	2	[91]	0	5	5	
Performance	19	0	[19]	1	0	1	.
Plain(e)	1	0	1	0	3	[3]	Only as contraction for "complain". No other usages.
Plea	6	4	[10]	1	0	1	

Table 1: Shakespeare-Daniel Raw Vocabulary Comparison (Pt 2)

Vocabulary Word	Shakespeare			Daniel			notes
	Plays	Poems	Total	Plays	Poems	Total	
Process	19	0	[19]	0	0	0	
Rated	16	0	[16]	1	2	3	
Rate	35	3	[38]	6	7	13	
Scorn	91	11	[102]	1	5	6	
Scorned	12	1	[13]	2	0	2	
Scorns	18	1	[19]	0	0	0	
Wasting	3	1	[4]	0	1	1	
Waste	41	8	[49]	2	5	7	
Wastes	2	2	4	0	4	4	
Way (Weigh)	44	3	[47]	5	8	13	
Withholds	4	0	[4]	0	0	0	
Withhold	8	1	[9]	2	0	2	
Wrought	34	5	39	24	65	[89]	
Yield	141	14	[155]	0	23	23	

As the reader can see, all but two words and one exact phrase are more common in the works of Shakespeare. Daniel used the word "wrought" and the exact phrase "dearly bought" more than Shakespeare. He also used the word "plaine" more often than Shakespeare as a shortened poetical usage for "complain". Regarding the two words ending in "-eth" suffixes, neither poet had ever used them elsewhere. Of all the words, however, Shakespeare used the specific word more often in 23 of 29 instances.

But the numbers must be adjusted in order to give a legitimate outcome. A far more important difference between the texts of the two authors is that fact that Shakespeare's poems and plays amount to roughly twice the total word count of Daniel's. This being the case, I provide, on Table 1A, a comparison of Shakespeare's raw numbers against twice Daniel's raw word count. This is more of an apples-to-apples comparison and much more indicative than the raw word counts.

This done, Daniel now shows slightly more use of "abated" and the near-match "wastes" (close to the word "wasting" in the poem). Even after doubling Daniel's word counts, however, Shakespeare still shows a higher use of 21 of the 29 words/phrases. Daniel has the higher count in 5 of 29. If we count only exact word/phrase matches, Shakespeare shows higher use in 16 of 22 instances, Daniel 4 of 22. Statistical analysis of the vocabulary of Sonnet 16, this is to say, argues heavily for the authorship of Shakespeare over Daniel.

Table 1A: Shakespeare–Danielx2 Raw Vocabulary Comparison (Pt. 1)

Vocabulary Word	Shakespeare			Daniel			Notes
	Plays	Poems	Total	Plays	Poems	Total	
Abated	3	0	3	2	2	[4]	
[Abate]	13	1	[14]	2	8	10	
Action	112	5	[117]	20	48	68	
Bought	52	1	[53]	4	12	16	
[Dearly bought]	1	0	1	4	6	[10]	
Dearly	32	1	[33]	14	12	26	
Excludeth	0	0	0	0	0	0	
Flat	29	0	[29]	2	4	6	Neither has "flat" for "flatly"
Hurt	84	4	[88]	32	24	56	
Lasting	12	4	[16]	2	12	14	
Overruleth	0	0	0	0	0	0	
Performance	19	0	[19]	2	0	2	
Perceive	89	2	[91]	0	10	10	
Plain[e]	1	0	1	0	6	[6]	Only as contraction for "complain". No other usages.
Plea	6	4	[10]	1	0	1	

Table 1A: Shakespeare-Danielx2 Raw Vocabulary Comparison (Pt. 2)

Vocabulary Word	Shakespeare			Daniel			Notes
	Plays	Poems	Total	Plays	Poems	Total	
Process	19	0	[19]	0	0	0	
Rated	16	0	[16]	2	4	6	
Rate	35	3	[38]	12	14	26	
Scorn	91	11	[102]	2	10	12	
Scorned	12	1	[13]	4	0	4	
Scorns	18	1	[19]	0	0	0	
Waste	41	8	[49]	4	10	14	
Wastes	2	2	4	0	8	[8]	
Wasting	3	1	[4]	0	2	2	
Way (Weigh)	44	3	[47]	10	16	26	
Withholds	4	0	[4]	0	0	0	
Withhold	8	1	[9]	4	0	4	
Wrought	34	5	39	48	130	[178]	
Yield	141	14	[155]	0	46	46	

However much statistical analysis strongly points to Shakespeare over Daniel as the author of the sonnet, another consideration argues for Shakespeare above *all* others. As has long been noted, Shakespeare creatively used legal terminology in his poems and plays far more often and at far greater length than any other creative writer of his time. While this is not quite as perfect a marker as the word "arbitrement," it is a key trait of Shakespeare to the exclusion of all others.

Returning to Sonnet 16, I provide italics for the words and phrases that are given a legal usage.

> *Way but the cause,* and give me leave to plaine me,
> For all my hurt, that my harts Queene hath wrought it,
> Shee whom I love so deare, the more to paine me,
> *Withholds my right, where I have dearely bought it.*
> *Dearely I bought* that was so *highly rated,*
> Even with the price of bloud and bodies wasting,
> *Shee would not yeeld that ought might be abated,*
> For all shee saw my Love was pure and lasting.
> And yet now scornes *performance of the passion,*
> And with hir presence *Justice overruleth,*
> Shee tels me flat hir beauty *beares no action,*
> And so my *plee and proces shee excludeth*:
> What wrong shee doth, the world may well perceive it,
> To accept my faith at first, and then to leave it.

The sonnet is little more than a discussion of the author's legal rights vis-a-vis his beloved given that he has lawfully paid the market price (and much more) for her passion. She has accepted the payment but refuses the performance. The poet now pleads his case to the reader as a judge or member of the jury hearing his civil case in court. He has lawfully bought the passion. The performance of it is due to him. Not only has the seller failed to deliver, but she won't yield in the slightest in order to abate the degree of the tort which she has forced him to bear under civil law. She won't even admit that the contract falls within the purview of a civil court action.

We have another example of a Shakespeare sonnet (this one happier) that uses legal terminology and civil law in a similar spirit.

Mine eye and heart are at a mortal war,
How to divide the conquest of thy sight;
Mine eye my heart thy picture's sight would *bar*,
My heart mine eye *the freedom of that right*,
My heart doth plead, that thou in him dost lie,
(A closet never pierc'd with crystal eyes,)
But *the defendant doth that plea deny*,
And says in him thy fair appearance lies.
To 'cide this title is impannelled
A quest of thoughts, all tenants to the heart;
And by their verdict is determined
The clear *eye's moiety, and the dear heart's part*:
As thus; mine eye's due is thine outward part
And *my heart's right* thine inward love of heart.[33]

Here there is a dispute, between eye and heart, over how to determine the proper rights of each at law. The heart being unable to love without the agency of the eye, the eye claims the greater rights. The eye being unable to love what it sees without the agency of the heart, the heart claims the greater part. An inquest is empanelled. A finding is issued. Possession of the outward part is given to the eye, possession of the inward to the heart. This kind of pervasive legal imagery is everywhere throughout Shakespeare and rarely to be found throughout *all other poets of the time combined.*

The source and handling of the imagery in both these sonnets is identical. More still, Samuel Daniel never developed imagery along these or similar lines. A statistical expression of this disparity is clear in Table 2, below, comparing legal usage.

Here we see that the strongest claim for Daniel remains his more common use of the exact phrase "dearly bought," in which "dearly" infers "at above market price" and "bought" describes a purchase providing the purchaser with rights of possession. It bears mentioning that the legal implications of "bought" only reveal themselves in an overall legal context. The word "dearly" only finds legal shading being an adverb modifying a verb/action having legal definition. Poets and the generality of their readers use them both far more often as terms of general usage, without a thought for the fact that they are terms that bear a legal definition within a

---

[33] Shakespeare. *Poems.* Sonnet 46 @ 169.

legal setting. This to highlight the fact that, for all these words are counted toward legal vocabulary, Daniel does not use the words or phrase in a legal context. I only include them here in order to be scrupulously fair. At bottom, buying and selling are acts established under civil law.

Daniel uses the exact expression 3 times (which we double to count as 6 times, here) to Shakespeare's 1. While it is not necessary to mention — the overwhelming preponderance of the statistical evidence being in the favor of Shakespeare — Shakespeare does use numerous other close variations on "dearly bought": i.e. "tendered dearly," "dearly hired," etc. Daniel more often uses the exact phrase. Both use variations upon the phrase in roughly equal measure.

Otherwise, the mere fact of the legal basis of the imagery weighs heavily in favor of Shakespeare. To this the statistical evidence further weighs in his favor. Of the 15 words/phrases, Shakespeare more commonly exhibits legal usage in 11 instances through his works, Daniel in 2. Daniel's usages are never part of an overall legal imagery in a poem or passage. They appear as isolated instances.

Table 2: Shakespeare-Danlelx2 Legal Usage Comparison [Pt 1]

Vocabulary Word	Shakespeare (plays/poems=Total)			Daniel (short poems/War=Total)			notes
	Plays	Poems	Total	Plays	Poems	Total	
Abated	1	0	[1]	0	0	0	
Abate	1	0	[1]	0	0	0	
Action	6	0	[6]	0	0	0	Legal action only.
Bought	52	1	[53]	4	12	16	All usages suggest legal transfer of product or service for money, with attendant legal rights.
Dearly bought	1	0	1	2	6	[8]	Shakespeare: Tender dearly [2], dearly hired, dearly paid, and other variations.
Dearly	9	0	9	6	10	[16]	At very high price.
Performance	4	0	[4]	0	0	0	Actual act of providing contracted product or service.

Table 2: Shakespeare-Danielx2 Legal Usage Comparison [Pt 2]

Vocabulary Word	Shakespeare (plays/poems=Total)			Daniel (short poems/War=Total)			notes
	Plays	Poems	Total	Plays	Poems	Total	
Plea	5	4	[9]	0	0	0	
Process	5	0	[5]	0	0	0	Legal process only.
Rated	8	0	[8]	0	2	2	Priced, market valued.
Rate	24	1	[25]	8	10	18	Price, market value
Way (Weigh)	6	1	[7]	0	6	6	You are right justice and you weigh this well... *2 Henry IV*
Withhold	0	0	0	0	0	0	
Withholds (my right)	0	0	0	0	0	0	...rights so forcibly withheld... *K. John*
Yield	23	0	[23]	0	12	12	Turn over some or all of a product or service without specific court order.

To add still more to the relationship between these usages and the work of Shakespeare, we may add two examples of precisely the identical usage. First, regarding the phrase "Withholds my right," the following from The Life and Death of King John (I. i.):

> The proud control of fierce and bloody war,
> To enforce these *rights so forcibly withheld.*

Next regarding the phrase "[Weigh] but the cause," this from 2 Henry IV (V. ii.):

> You are right, justice, and *you weigh this well;*
> Therefore still bear the balance and the sword:...

Shakespeare does yield other references to the balance and weighing of causes, associated with the law, but this is the most precise match. No similar usage is to be found in the works of Daniel.

With all of this by way of quantifiable textual evidence, there can be little doubt the sonnet was written by William Shakespeare. Add the use of "arbitrement" elsewhere in nearby texts, and the provenance of the poems in question, and I feel entirely justified to declare that Sonnet 16 from the "sundry other rare Sonnets of divers Noble men and Gentlemen," appended to the end of the 1591 edition of *Astrophel and Stella,* was written by William Shakespeare.

A Final Comparison

But we have not yet exhausted our evidence. There is still the passage, mentioned above, from Shakespeare's *Venus and Adonis* which would be entered in the Stationers' Registers in April of 1593 for publication some year and a half later and therefore was very possibly in-progress in 1591[34].

> Pure lips, sweet seals in my soft lips imprinted,
> What bargains may I make, still to be sealing?"
> To sell myself I can be well contented,
> So thou wilt buy, and pay, and use good dealing.
> What purchase if you make for fear of slips,
> Set thy seal-manual on my wax-red lips.[35]

Here again we have sealing with a kiss. But far more to the point, we have a "bargain," a civil contract, in which Venus "can be well contented". Here is a bargain which the lover wishes to go through with the performance of the service purchased. Less imperious than the lover in Sonnet 16, Venus wants a market relationship with Adonis, arranges the purchase, the sealing of the bargain and asks to be allowed to perform the passion she is all too willing to perform. The imagery is identical to that in Sonnet 16.

Unfortunately, we cannot be equally sure when Sonnet 16 was actually written, only when it was published. There is reason to think that Sonnet 3, among the "sundry other rare Sonnets," which I also claim was likely written by Shakespeare, and which I will address in future studies, may have been written considerably earlier than 1591. Sonnet 12, which seems even more likely by the Bard, may show signs of having been written shortly before it was published. Only another round of close textual study will tell if the impression is correct or if any approximate date can be

---

[34] See my "Shake-speare's Greek", on canonical Shakespeare Sonnets 153 & 154 and *Venus and Adonis*. Virtual Grub Street, May 8, 2014. http://gilbertwesleypurdy.blogspot.com/2014/05/shake-speares-greek.html.

[35] Shakespeare. *Poems* @ 26.

assigned at all. All of this being the case, a roughly equal date of composition for both Sonnet 16 and *Venus and Adonis* must remain conjectural for now. The above stanza from *Venus and Adonis* suggests that it might have been written at about the same time.

A Brief Epilogue

While this monograph by no means addresses all the Shakespeare matters relating to the "other rare sonnets of divers Noble men and Gentlemen," at the end of the1591 *Astrophel and Stella*, it seems wise to limit ourselves here to a detailed analysis of Sonnet 16 alone. It is best to start with the "slam dunk" and not to dilute its case by trying to accomplish too much at once.

Sonnets 3 and 12 are also prime candidates for the pen of Shakespeare. Sonnet 3 shares the Bard's stylistic traits in a more general way and his use of Phoenix imagery. But the same can be said of Sonnet XXXVIII (38) from Samuel Daniel's *Delia* for all certain other tendencies are not, to the best of my knowledge, shared by Daniel.

Sonnet 3

> THe only bird alone that Nature frames,
> When weary of the tedious life shee lives,
> By fier dies, yet finds new life in flames,
> Hir ashes to hir shape new essence gives.
> When onely I the onely wretched wight,
> Wearie of life that breaths but sorrows blasts,
> Pursues the flame of such a beautie bright,
> That burnes my heart, and yet my life still lasts.
> O Soveraigne light that with thy sacred flame
> Consumes my life, revive me after this,
> And make me (with the happie bird) the same
> That dies to live, by favour of thy blisse.
> This deede of thine shall shew a Goddesse power,
> In so long death, to grant one living hower.

In Shakespeare's "Phoenix and the Turtle," the Phoenix is also the turtle-dove's "queen". But Daniel refers both to Queen Elizabeth and to his lover as "queen". He refers to Elizabeth, James I and his lover as "soveraigne". The differences between the two styles and vocabularies are subtle and would make this monograph even more difficult to follow. The threads of the analysis of Sonnet 16 would be lost track of in an even greater tangle of historical and textual strands.

Sonnet 12 is even more promising.

> THe tablet of my heavie fortunes heere
> Upon thine Altare (Paphian Power) I place;
> The greevous shipwracke of my travels deere
> In bulged barke, all perisht in disgrace.
> That traitor Love, was Pilot to my woe,
> My Sailes were hope, spread with my sighs of griefe,
> The twinelights which my haples course did show,
> Hard by th'inconstant sands of false reliefe,
> Where two bright starres which led my view apart,
> A Sirens voice allur'd me come so neare,
> To perish on the marble of her hart,
> A danger which my soule did never feare:
> Lo thus he fares that trusts a calme too much;
> And thus fare I whose credit hath beene such.

Shakespeare's sonnets CLIII (153) and CLIV (154) are generally accepted by scholars to have been associated with a trip by the Court of Elizabeth I, in 1592, to the baths at Bath, England. In them, he compares Bath to the sacred baths at Paphos.[36] We also find the "sailes" and "barque" of the Rival Poet sonnets, which I have assigned elsewhere to about this time.[37] Again, the proximity of time between the publication of Sonnet 12 and the Shakespeare sonnets adds to the force of the connection. Daniel seems to have no similarly exact connection to the imagery here.

Then, of course, there is the matter of the "Canto Quinto". The breathtaking use of "arbitrement" almost argues the pen of Shakespeare in itself. But there is the deadly debate over the Shakespeare Authorship Question and it would surely take over this humble little bark (to use a

---

[36] See my "Shake-speare's Greek". (http://gilbertwesleypurdy.blogspot.com/2014/05/shake-speares-greek.html)

[37] Purdy, *Was Shake-speare Gay?*

favorite image of the Bard) and dash it to pieces against the polemical rocks. These are matters each deserving their own separate treatments, in their proper places.

Bibliography/List of Works Cited

Campion, Thomas, *Booke of Ayres*. London: Peter Short, 1601. Reprinted in *Campion's Works*, ed. Percival Vivian. Oxford: Clarendon Press, 1909. 1-30.

Campion, Thomas. *Campion's Works*, ed. Percival Vivian. Oxford: Clarendon Press, 1909.

Clark, Mary Cowden. *The Complete Concordance to Shakespeare*. London: Bickers and Son, 1878.

Daniel, Samuel. *Delia. Contayning certayne sonnets: with The complaint of Rosamond*. Ed. John Payne Collier. London: T. Richards, 1870(?)

Daniel, Samuel. *The Complete Works in Verse and Prose of Samuel Daniel*. Ed. Alexander Grossart. 5 vols. Privately Printed, 1885.

Davis, Frank. "The Poem Grief of Minde: Who Wrote It?" The Oxfordian, Volume V (2002): 159-73.

Dowland, John. *Second Book of Songes or Ayres*. London: George Eastland, 1600. XI.

Englands Parnassus, Compiled by Robert Allot, 1600, ed. Charles Crawford. Oxford: Clarendon, 1913.

Fraunce, Abraham. *Victoria: a Latin Comedy*, ed. G. E. Moore Smith. London: David McNutt, 1906.

Furness, Mrs. Horace Howard. *A Concordance to Shakespeare's Poems*. Philadelphia: Lippincott and Co., 1875.

The Fuller's Worthies Library. Ed. Alexander Grossart. 4 vols. Privately printed, 1876. "The Poems of Thomas Lord Vaux: Edward Earl of Oxford: Robert Earl of Essex: Walter Earl of Essex." Miscellanies. Vol. 4.

Nashe, Thomas. *The Complete Works of Thomas Nashe*, 6 vols. Ed. Alexander Grossart. Privately Printed, 1883-1885.

Notes and Queries, Tenth Series, Volume IX. July – December, 1908.

Purdy, Gilbert Wesley. "Shake-speare's Greek". Virtual Grub Street, May 8, 2014. (http://gilbertwesleypurdy.blogspot.com/2014/05/shake-speares-greek.html)

Purdy, Gilbert Wesley. *Was Shake-speare Gay? Straight Male Scholarly Angst and Shake-speare's Sonnets.* Richmond, VA: The Virtual Vanaprastha, 2014.

Sams, Eric and Matthews, Robert. "On the use of Thisted & Efron's technique to determine authorship."
http://ericsams.org/index.php/shakespeare-archive/essays-and-reviews-unpubl/262-on-the-use-of-thisted-efron-s-technique-to-determine-authorship.

Shakespeare, William. *The poems of Shakespeare.* Ed. Alexander Dyce. London: Bell and Daldy, 1857.

Sidney, Sir Philip, *Syr P.S. His Astrophel and Stella. Wherein the excellence of sweete poesie is concluded. To the end of which are added, sundry other rare sonnets of divers noble men and gentlemen.* Intro. by Thomas Nashe. London: Thomas Newman, 1591. Ann Arbor, MI ; Oxford (UK) :: Text Creation Partnership, 2003-01 (EEBO-TCP Phase 1).

Sidney, Sir Philip. *The Complete Poems of Sir Philip Sidney.* 2 vols. Ed. Alexander Grossart. Privately Printed, 1873.

Thisted, Ronald and Efron, Bradley. "Did Shakespeare Write a Newly Discovered Poem?" Technical Report No. 111. Stanford, California: Stanford Universtiy, April 1986.
https://statistics.stanford.edu/sites/default/files/BIO%20111.pdf

Made in the USA
Lexington, KY
06 August 2018